low fat

simple and delicious easy-to-make recipes

Susanna Tee

p

This is a Parragon Publishing Book
First published in 2003

Parragon Publishing
Queen Street House
4 Queen Street
Bath, BA1 1HE, UK

ISBN: 1-40542-532-6

Printed in China

Produced by the Bridgewater Book Company Ltd.

Photographer Ian Parsons

Home Economist Sara Hesketh

NOTES FOR THE READER

- This book uses both imperial and metric measurements. Follow the same units of measurement throughout; do not mix imperial and metric.

- All spoon measurements are level: teaspoons are assumed to be 5 ml, and tablespoons are assumed to be 15 ml.

- Unless otherwise stated, milk is assumed to be whole milk, eggs and individual vegetables such as carrots are medium, and pepper is freshly ground black pepper.

- Recipes using raw eggs should be avoided by infants, the elderly, pregnant women, convalescents, and anyone suffering from an illness.

- The times given are an approximate guide only. Preparation times differ according to the techniques used by different people and the cooking times may also vary from those given. Optional ingredients, variations, or serving suggestions have not been included in the calculations.

contents

introduction

This book will convince you that a lowfat diet need never be dreary. These healthy dishes are bursting with flavor. All are easy to prepare and good to eat. There are no complicated cooking methods involved or expensive ingredients to buy.

The recipes use fat-free or fat-reduced cooking methods, and all you need to do is to select lowfat dairy products, lean meats, such as skinless chicken and turkey, and the leanest cuts of beef, lamb, and pork, and of course, plenty of vegetables.

Vegetable oil spray also reduces the amount of fat used, for example when stir-frying, and nonstick liner is useful for lining cookie sheets. The only special equipment you need is a heavy, nonstick skillet or a nonstick wok.

When serving bread or vegetables with these dishes, don't be tempted to reach for the butter dish: simply eat delicious fresh bread and add a generous sprinkling of chopped herbs to the vegetables. Instead of rich salad dressings, make your own with lowfat yogurt or cottage cheese, or use a fat-reduced mayonnaise. You will soon be feeling healthier without feeling deprived of your favorite dishes.

guide to recipe key	
easy	Recipes are graded as follows: 1 pea = easy; 2 peas = very easy; 3 peas = extremely easy.
serves 4	Recipes generally serve four people. Simply halve the ingredients to serve two, taking care not to mix imperial and metric measurements.
10 minutes	Preparation time. Where chilling is involved, this time has been added on separately: eg, 15 minutes + 1 hour to chill.
10 minutes	Cooking time.

greek feta salad
page 16

marinated lamb kabobs
page 56

cheese & spinach lasagna
page 64

raspberry creams
page 92

light lunches & suppers

These are recipes that are easy to make yet satisfying to eat at a midday break or as a light evening meal. They are ideal served simply with fresh crusty bread and then followed with fresh fruit for a lowfat, healthy lunch or supper. Most of them—for example, Sweet Red Bell Pepper & Tomato Soup, and Greek Feta Salad can also be served as an appetizer as they are light and refreshing. Choose from delicious temptations such as Chilled Smoked Mackerel with Horseradish Dressing, Shrimp & Mango Salad, and Vegetable Frittata.

sweet red bell pepper
& tomato soup

	ingredients	
extremely easy	1 tbsp olive oil	14 oz/400 g canned
	2 tbsp water	chopped tomatoes
serves 4	2 red bell peppers, deseeded and chopped finely	5 cups vegetable bouillon
	1 garlic clove, chopped finely	salt and pepper
5 minutes	1 onion, chopped finely	fresh basil leaves, to garnish
30–35 minutes		

NUTRITIONAL INFORMATION

calories	89
protein	3 g
carbohydrate	12 g
sugars	10 g
fat	4 g
saturates	0.5 g

Put the oil, water, bell peppers, garlic, and onion in a pan, heat gently, and cook for 5–10 minutes, or until the vegetables have softened. Cover the pan and simmer for a further 10 minutes.

Add the tomatoes, bouillon, salt, and pepper and simmer, uncovered, for 15 minutes.

Serve garnished with basil leaves.

mixed bean soup

	ingredients	
extremely easy	1 garlic clove, crushed	salt and pepper
	1 onion, chopped finely	pinch of dried mixed herbs
	1 celery stalk, sliced finely	14 oz/400 g canned red kidney beans,
serves 4	1 carrot, diced finely	drained and rinsed
	1 leek, sliced finely	14 oz/400 g black-eye peas, drained
	14 oz/400 g canned	and rinsed
10 minutes	chopped tomatoes	
	2½ cups vegetable bouillon	warm crusty bread, to serve
35 minutes		

NUTRITIONAL
INFORMATION

calories	238
protein	16 g
carbohydrate	42 g
sugars	11 g
fat	2 g
saturates	neg

Put all the ingredients, except the beans, into a large pan. Bring to a boil, then simmer for 30 minutes, stirring occasionally, until the vegetables are tender.

Add the beans and simmer for a further 4–5 minutes, or until hot.

Serve with warm crusty bread.

chicken & vegetable soup

		ingredients	
extremely easy		1 onion, chopped finely 1 garlic clove, chopped finely 1¼ cups shredded white cabbage 2 medium carrots, chopped finely 4 potatoes, diced 1 green bell pepper, deseeded and diced 14 oz/400 g canned chopped tomatoes	5⅔ cups chicken bouillon salt and pepper 1¼ cups diced cooked chicken chopped fresh parsley, to garnish warm crusty bread, to serve
serves 4			
10 minutes			
1 hour 10 minutes			

NUTRITIONAL
INFORMATION

calories	240
protein	19 g
carbohydrate	37 g
sugars	10 g
fat	3 g
saturates	0.5 g

Put all the ingredients, except the chicken and parsley, in a large pan and bring to a boil. Simmer for 1 hour, or until the vegetables are tender.

Add the chicken and simmer for a further 10 minutes, or until hot.

Garnish with parsley and serve with warm crusty bread.

tuna & fresh vegetable salad

extremely easy

serves 4

10 minutes + 1 hour to marinate

—

ingredients

DRESSING
4 tbsp reduced-calorie mayonnaise
4 tbsp lowfat plain yogurt
2 tbsp white wine vinegar
salt and pepper

12 cherry tomatoes, halved
1½ cups whole green beans,
    cut into 1 inch/2.5 cm pieces

8 oz/225 g zucchini, sliced thinly
3¼ cups thinly sliced
    white mushrooms
12 oz/350 g canned tuna in brine,
    drained and flaked

chopped fresh parsley, to garnish

salad greens, to serve

NUTRITIONAL
INFORMATION

calories	187
protein	26 g
carbohydrate	8 g
sugars	7 g
fat	6 g
saturates	0.5 g

To make the dressing, put the mayonnaise, yogurt, vinegar, salt, and pepper in a screw-topped jar and shake together until the ingredients are well blended.

Put the tomatoes, beans, zucchini, and mushrooms in a bowl. Pour over the dressing and marinate for about 1 hour.

To serve, arrange the salad greens on a serving dish. Add the vegetables and then the tuna, and garnish with chopped parsley.

greek feta salad

extremely easy	
serves 4	
10 minutes	
—	

ingredients

DRESSING
3 tbsp extra virgin olive oil
1 tbsp lemon juice
½ tsp dried oregano
salt and pepper

4 tomatoes, sliced
½ cucumber, peeled and sliced
1 small red onion, sliced thinly
4 oz/115 g feta cheese, cubed
8 black olives

a few grape leaves, to serve

NUTRITIONAL
INFORMATION

calories	186
protein	6 g
carbohydrate	7 g
sugars	6 g
fat	15 g
saturates	5 g

To make the dressing, put the oil, lemon juice, oregano, salt, and pepper in a screw-topped jar and shake together until blended.

Arrange the grape leaves on a serving dish and then the tomatoes, cucumber, and onion. Sprinkle the cheese and olives on top. Pour the dressing over the salad and serve.

shrimp & mango salad

extremely easy	
serves 4	
10 minutes	
—	

ingredients

2 mangoes
2 cups peeled, cooked shrimp

DRESSING
juice from the mangoes
6 tbsp lowfat plain yogurt
2 tbsp reduced-calorie mayonnaise
1 tbsp lemon juice
salt and pepper

4 whole cooked shrimp, to garnish

salad greens, to serve

NUTRITIONAL
INFORMATION

calories	146
protein	16 g
carbohydrate	15 g
sugars	14 g
fat	3 g
saturates	0.5 g

Cutting close to the pit, cut a large slice from one side of each mango, then cut another slice from the opposite side. Without breaking the skin, cut the flesh in the segments into squares, then push the skin inside out to expose the cubes, and cut away from the skin. Use a sharp knife to peel the remaining center section and cut the flesh away from the pit into cubes. Reserve any juice in a bowl and put the mango flesh in a separate bowl.

Add the shrimp to the mango flesh. Add the yogurt, mayonnaise, lemon juice, salt, and pepper to the juice and blend together.

Arrange the salad greens on a serving dish and add the mango flesh and shrimp. Pour the dressing over them and serve garnished with the whole shrimp.

warm chicken liver salad

		ingredients	
very easy		salad greens	1 tsp chopped fresh tarragon
		1 tbsp olive oil	1 tsp wholegrain mustard
serves 4		1 small onion, chopped finely	2 tbsp balsamic vinegar
		1 lb/450 g frozen chicken livers, thawed	salt and pepper
5 minutes			
10–12 minutes			

NUTRITIONAL INFORMATION

calories	142
protein	21 g
carbohydrate	2 g
sugars	1 g
fat	6 g
saturates	1 g

Arrange the salad greens on serving plates.

Heat the oil in a nonstick skillet, add the onion, and cook for 5 minutes, or until softened. Add the chicken livers, tarragon, and mustard and cook for 3–5 minutes, stirring, until tender. Put on top of the salad greens.

Add the vinegar, salt, and pepper to the skillet and heat, stirring constantly, until all the sediment has been lifted from the skillet. Pour the dressing over the chicken livers and serve warm.

chilled smoked mackerel
with horseradish dressing

		ingredients
	extremely easy	4 smoked mackerel
	serves 4	DRESSING $2/3$ cup lowfat plain yogurt
	10 minutes + at least 30 minutes to chill	1 tsp grated horseradish salt and pepper
	—	watercress sprigs or mizuna, ` to garnish

NUTRITIONAL INFORMATION

calories	376
protein	21 g
carbohydrate	3 g
sugars	3 g
fat	31 g
saturates	6 g

Remove the skin from the mackerel fillets, then cut each fillet in half lengthwise. Chill in the refrigerator for at least 30 minutes.

Meanwhile, combine the yogurt, horseradish, salt, and pepper. Chill in the refrigerator with the mackerel.

To serve, arrange the mackerel on serving plates, spoon the horseradish dressing over it, and garnish with watercress sprigs or mizuna.

vegetable frittata

easy	
serves 4	
10 minutes	
20–30 minutes	

ingredients

4 eggs
2 egg whites
salt and pepper
1 tsp olive oil
1 onion, chopped coarsely
1 garlic clove, chopped finely

1 green bell pepper, deseeded and
    chopped finely
1 zucchini, sliced thickly
8 oz/225 g cooked potatoes, diced
1 tomato, chopped coarsely
½ cup grated reduced-fat mozzarella

NUTRITIONAL
INFORMATION

calories	215
protein	13 g
carbohydrate	15 g
sugars	5 g
fat	12 g
saturates	4 g

Beat the whole eggs and egg whites in a bowl and season with salt and pepper.

Heat the oil in a large nonstick skillet and add the onion, garlic, and green bell pepper. Cook for 5 minutes, or until softened. Add the zucchini and potatoes and cook for a further 5–10 minutes, or until lightly browned. Stir in the tomato.

Pour in the egg mixture and cook over low heat for 5–10 minutes, or until the mixture is set and only the top is runny. Sprinkle the cheese over the top.

Transfer the pan to a preheated broiler and cook until the top is set, but not hard, and the cheese has melted and begun to brown. Serve hot, cut into wedges.

homemade
turkey burgers

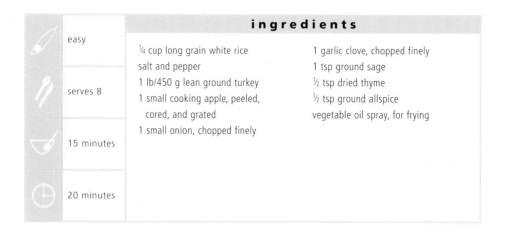

easy	
serves 8	
15 minutes	
20 minutes	

ingredients

¼ cup long grain white rice
salt and pepper
1 lb/450 g lean ground turkey
1 small cooking apple, peeled,
  cored, and grated
1 small onion, chopped finely

1 garlic clove, chopped finely
1 tsp ground sage
½ tsp dried thyme
½ tsp ground allspice
vegetable oil spray, for frying

**NUTRITIONAL
INFORMATION**

calories	161
protein	26 g
carbohydrate	10 g
sugars	5 g
fat	2 g
saturates	1 g

Cook the rice in a large pan of boiling salted water for about 10 minutes, or until tender. Drain, rinse under cold running water, then drain well again.

Put the cooked rice and all the remaining ingredients in a large bowl and mix well together. With wet hands, shape the mixture into 8 thick burgers.

Spray a large, nonstick skillet with oil, add the burgers, and cook for about 10 minutes, turning them over several times, until they are golden brown. Remove from the skillet and serve while hot.

main courses

The following recipes show just how easy it is to prepare lowfat dishes. They all use lean cuts of meat, poultry, and fish that are seasoned with fresh vegetables, herbs, and spices, and are packed with flavor. There are recipes for family meals and entertaining, and recipes for warm summer evenings or cold winter's nights. Choose from such dishes as Moussaka, Chicken with a Honey Glazed Crust, Marinated Lamb Kabobs, and Broiled Salmon with Red Bell Pepper Sauce. All are mouthwatering—the only difficulty is deciding which to choose!

mexican chicken burritos

very easy	
serves 4	
10 minutes	
30 minutes	

ingredients

8 wheat flour tortillas
vegetable oil spray
1 onion, chopped finely
4 skinless, boneless chicken breast
  portions, sliced thinly

1 packet taco seasoning
4 tomatoes, chopped coarsely
4 scallions, sliced thinly

1 tub tomato salsa, to serve

**NUTRITIONAL
INFORMATION**

calories	473
protein	40 g
carbohydrate	75 g
sugars	7 g
fat	4 g
saturates	1 g

Preheat the oven to 300°F/150°C.

Wrap the tortillas in aluminum foil and cook in the oven for
10 minutes, or until soft.

Meanwhile, spray a large nonstick skillet with oil. Add the onion
and cook for 5 minutes, or until softened. Add the chicken.
Stirring occasionally, cook for 5 minutes, or until tender. Stir in
the taco seasoning.

Preheat the oven to 350°F/180°C. Put the chicken mixture in the
center of each tortilla and add the tomatoes and scallions. Fold
the tortillas into a packet and put in an ovenproof dish.

Cover the dish and cook in the preheated oven for 20 minutes.
Spoon the tomato salsa over the hot tortillas before serving.

chicken with
a honey-glazed crust

		ingredients
very easy		3 tbsp wheat germ
		3 tbsp honey
serves 4		1 tbsp French mustard
		4 skinless chicken breast portions
5 minutes		salad greens (optional), to serve
30–40 minutes		

NUTRITIONAL INFORMATION

calories	194
protein	31 g
carbohydrate	13 g
sugars	12 g
fat	2 g
saturates	0.5 g

Preheat the oven to 375°F/190°C.

Put the wheat germ, honey, and mustard in a bowl and mix well together. Put the chicken breast portions on a cookie sheet and spread with the honey mixture.

Bake the chicken in the oven for 30–40 minutes, or until the chicken is tender and a crust has formed. Remove from the oven and transfer to warm serving dishes.

Serve with salad greens, if you like.

italian braised
chicken & fennel

		ingredients
	very easy	4 tomatoes, chopped finely
		1 garlic clove, crushed
	serves 4	¼ cup white wine
		2 tsp balsamic vinegar
		salt and pepper
		4 skinless chicken breast portions
	5 minutes	4 small fennel bulbs, quartered
		flat leaf parsley, to garnish
	35 minutes	

NUTRITIONAL INFORMATION

calories	166
protein	32 g
carbohydrate	5 g
sugars	5 g
fat	2 g
saturates	0.5 g

Put the tomatoes, garlic, wine, vinegar, salt, and pepper in a large, nonstick skillet and bring to a boil. Reduce the heat and add the chicken and fennel pieces. Cover and simmer for about 30 minutes, or until the chicken and fennel are tender.

Using a slotted spoon, transfer the chicken and fennel to warm serving plates.

Bring the sauce to a boil and cook, stirring occasionally, until thickened slightly. Spoon the sauce over the chicken and serve garnished with parsley.

tandoori chicken

		ingredients	
very easy		4–8 skinless chicken portions	1 tsp garam masala
			½ tsp salt
		MARINADE	½ tsp cayenne pepper, optional
serves 4		1 small onion, quartered	2 tbsp lemon or lime juice
		2 garlic cloves	4 tbsp lowfat plain yogurt
		1 tsp chopped fresh ginger	¼ tsp red food coloring
10 minutes + 24 hours to marinate		2 tsp ground cumin	
		2 tsp ground coriander	lemon or lime wedges, to garnish
45 minutes to 1 hour			

NUTRITIONAL INFORMATION

calories	160
protein	50 g
carbohydrate	4 g
sugars	3 g
fat	20 g
saturates	1 g

Using a sharp knife, cut ½ inch/1 cm deep slashes in each piece of chicken and put in a shallow dish.

Put all the remaining ingredients in a food processor and process until smooth. Spread the marinade over the chicken pieces, working it into the cuts in the flesh. Cover the dish and marinate in the refrigerator for 24 hours.

Preheat the oven to 400°F/200°C.

Place the chicken pieces on a rack in a roasting pan and cook in the oven for 45 minutes to 1 hour, turning the pieces over once and basting with the juices in the pan, until tender.

Serve garnished with lemon or lime wedges.

herb-crusted haddock
with tomato salsa

		ingredients	
	very easy	2 cups fresh white bread crumbs	vegetable oil spray
		3 tbsp lemon juice	4 haddock fillets
	serves 4	1 tbsp pesto sauce	
		2 tbsp chopped fresh parsley	1 tub tomato salsa, to serve
		salt and pepper	
	10 minutes		
	10–15 minutes		

NUTRITIONAL
INFORMATION

calories	245
protein	41 g
carbohydrate	16 g
sugars	2 g
fat	2 g
saturates	0 g

Put the bread crumbs, 2 tablespoons of the lemon juice, the pesto sauce, parsley, salt, and pepper in a bowl and mix well together.

Line a broiler pan with aluminum foil and spray with vegetable oil. Place the haddock fillets on the foil and sprinkle with the remaining tablespoon of lemon juice and more salt and pepper. Cook under a preheated broiler for 5 minutes.

Turn the haddock fillets over and spread the herb and bread crumb mixture over the top of each.

Cook for a further 5–10 minutes, or until the haddock is tender and the crust is golden brown.

Serve with the tomato salsa spooned over the top of each fish.

broiled salmon with red bell pepper sauce

	easy	
	serves 4	
	15 minutes	
	35–45 minutes	

ingredients

3 red bell peppers
vegetable oil spray
4 salmon steaks
1 tbsp lemon juice
salt and pepper

1 onion, chopped finely
1 garlic clove, chopped finely
2 tsp balsamic vinegar
handful of fresh basil leaves

NUTRITIONAL INFORMATION

calories	326
protein	32 g
carbohydrate	11 g
sugars	10 g
fat	17 g
saturates	3 g

Preheat the oven to 400°F/200°C.

Put the bell peppers on a cookie sheet and roast in the oven for 25 minutes, turning once, until deflated and slightly charred. Let cool, then peel off the skins and discard with the core and seeds.

Meanwhile, line a broiler pan with aluminum foil and spray with oil. Place the salmon steaks on the foil, sprinkle with lemon juice, salt, and pepper, and cook under a preheated broiler for 10–20 minutes, turning once, until tender.

Spray a small nonstick pan with oil and fry the onion and garlic for 5 minutes, or until softened. Process in a food processor with the bell pepper flesh, vinegar, basil, salt, and pepper until smooth. Return the mixture to the pan and reheat gently.

Serve the red bell pepper sauce with the cooked salmon steaks.

baked fish & fries

very easy	**ingredients**
serves 4	450 g/1 lb mealy potatoes, peeled and cut into thick, even French fries vegetable oil spray ½ cup all-purpose white flour 1 egg
20 minutes	1 cup fresh white bread crumbs, seasoned with salt and pepper 4 cod or haddock fillets
40–45 minutes	

NUTRITIONAL
INFORMATION

calories	322
protein	37 g
carbohydrate	37 g
sugars	1 g
fat	4 g
saturates	1 g

Preheat the oven to 400°F/200°C. Line 2 cookie sheets with nonstick liner.

Rinse the sliced potatoes under cold running water, then dry well on a clean dish towel. Put in a bowl, spray with oil, and toss together until coated. Spread the fries on a cookie sheet and cook in the oven for 40–45 minutes, turning once, until golden.

Meanwhile, put the flour on a plate, beat the egg in a shallow dish, and spread the seasoned bread crumbs on a large plate. Dip the fish fillets in the flour to coat, then the egg, letting any excess drip off, and finally the bread crumbs, patting them firmly into the fish. Place the fish in a single layer on a cookie sheet.

Fifteen minutes before the fries have cooked, bake the fish fillets in the oven for 10–15 minutes, turning them once during cooking, until the fish is tender. Serve the fish with the fries.

red snapper
with citrus fruit

		ingredients	
	very easy	MARINADE	vegetable oil spray, for frying
		6 tbsp fresh orange juice	4 red snapper
	serves 4	3 tbsp lemon juice	
		3 tbsp lime juice	orange segments, to garnish
		4 tbsp dry sherry	
	10 minutes + 4 hours to marinate	1 tsp chopped garlic	
		1 tsp chopped fresh ginger	
		salt and pepper	
	10–15 minutes		

NUTRITIONAL INFORMATION

calories	194
protein	28 g
carbohydrate	3 g
sugars	3 g
fat	6 g
saturates	0 g

Put all the marinade ingredients in a shallow dish and mix them well together.

Using a sharp knife, slash the snapper 3 times on each side. Add the fish to the marinade and marinate in the refrigerator, turning once or twice, for about 4 hours.

Line a broiler pan with aluminum foil and spray with vegetable oil. Place the fish on the foil and cook under a preheated broiler for 10–15 minutes, turning once and spooning over the marinade, until the flesh is tender.

Serve garnished with orange segments.

flounder packets
with fresh herbs

very easy	
serves 4	
10 minutes	
15 minutes	

ingredients

vegetable oil spray	finely grated rind and juice
4 flounder fillets, skinned	of 2 lemons
6 tbsp chopped fresh herbs,	1 small onion, sliced thinly
such as dill, parsley, chives,	1 tbsp capers, rinsed (optional)
thyme, or marjoram	salt and pepper

NUTRITIONAL
INFORMATION

calories	129
protein	25 g
carbohydrate	2 g
sugars	1 g
fat	2 g
saturates	0 g

Preheat the oven to 375°F/190°C. Cut 4 large squares of aluminum foil, each large enough to hold a fish and form a packet, and spray with oil.

Place each fish fillet on a foil sheet and sprinkle them with the herbs, lemon rind and juice, onion, capers (if using), salt. and pepper. Fold the foil to make a secure packet and place on a cookie sheet.

Bake the packets in the oven for 15 minutes, or until tender.

Serve the fish piping hot, in their loosely opened packets.

stir-fried beef
& snow peas

	very easy	
	serves 4	
	10 minutes	
	10 minutes	

ingredients

1 lb/450 g round or sirloin steak,
  sliced thinly
2 tbsp soy sauce
5 tbsp hoisin sauce
2 tbsp dry sherry
vegetable oil spray
1 onion, sliced thinly
1 tsp chopped fresh garlic
1 tsp chopped fresh ginger

1 carrot, sliced thinly
1 lb/450 g snow peas
8 oz/225 g canned sliced bamboo
  shoots, drained

fresh sprigs of cilantro, to garnish

cooked rice or noodles, to serve

NUTRITIONAL
INFORMATION

calories	249
protein	33 g
carbohydrate	15 g
sugars	12 g
fat	6 g
saturates	2 g

Put the strips of beef in a bowl, add the soy sauce, hoisin sauce, and sherry and stir together. Let marinate while you are cooking the vegetables.

Spray a large nonstick wok with oil. Add the onion, garlic, ginger, carrot, and snow peas and stir-fry for 5 minutes, or until softened.

Add the beef and marinade to the wok and stir-fry for 2–3 minutes, or until tender. Add the bamboo shoots and stir-fry for a further minute, until hot.

Transfer to a warm serving dish, garnish with cilantro, and serve with cooked rice or noodles, if you like.

bœuf stroganoff

very easy	
serves 4	
5 minutes	
15 minutes	

ingredients

vegetable oil spray
1 onion, sliced coarsely
3¼ cups thinly sliced
  white mushrooms
1 tsp French mustard
1 lb/450 g round or sirloin steak,
  sliced thinly

1¼ cups reduced-fat
  crème fraîche
salt and pepper

chopped fresh parsley, to garnish

NUTRITIONAL
INFORMATION

calories	302
protein	30 g
carbohydrate	7 g
sugars	5 g
fat	17 g
saturates	11 g

Spray a large, nonstick skillet with oil. Add the onion and cook, stirring, for 5 minutes, until softened and lightly colored.

Add the mushrooms and mustard to the skillet and cook, stirring occasionally, for a further 4–5 minutes, or until lightly colored.

Add the beef to the skillet and cook, stirring occasionally, for 5 minutes, or until tender. Add the crème fraîche and salt and pepper, then heat, stirring constantly, until hot.

Serve garnished with chopped parsley.

linguine with shrimp

		ingredients	
	very easy	12 oz/350 g linguine	1 tsp chopped fresh garlic
		salt and pepper	1 tsp chopped fresh ginger
		1 tbsp white wine vinegar	2 cups peeled cooked shrimp
	serves 4	1 tbsp lemon juice	4 scallions, sliced thinly
		2 tbsp tomato paste	
		pinch of sugar	chopped fresh parsley, to garnish
	5 minutes	6 tbsp water	
	15 minutes		

NUTRITIONAL
INFORMATION

calories	359
protein	21 g
carbohydrate	68 g
sugars	5 g
fat	2 g
saturates	0 g

Cook the pasta in a large pan of boiling salted water for 10 minutes, or as directed on the packet, until tender.

Meanwhile, put the vinegar, lemon juice, tomato paste, sugar, water, salt, and pepper in a bowl and mix together.

Put the garlic, ginger, shrimp, and scallions in a large, heavy nonstick skillet and heat gently for 1–2 minutes, stirring constantly, until hot.

Drain the cooked pasta and add to the skillet. Combine with the sauce mixture and heat, stirring, until the pasta is well coated and the sauce is heated through.

Serve garnished with chopped parsley.

moussaka

		ingredients	
easy		2 eggplants, sliced thinly	salt and pepper
		1 lb/450 g lean ground beef	2 eggs
serves 4		2 onions, sliced thinly	1¼ cups lowfat
		1 tsp finely chopped garlic	plain yogurt
		14 oz/400 g canned tomatoes	1 tbsp grated Parmesan cheese
40 minutes		2 tbsp chopped fresh parsley	
45 minutes			

NUTRITIONAL
INFORMATION

calories	357
protein	36 g
carbohydrate	17 g
sugars	15 g
fat	16 g
saturates	7 g

In a large nonstick skillet, dry-fry the eggplant slices, in batches, on both sides until brown. Remove from the skillet.

Add the beef to the pan and cook for 5 minutes, stirring, until browned. Stir in the onions and garlic and cook for 5 minutes, or until lightly browned. Add the tomatoes, parsley, salt, and pepper, then bring the mixture to a boil, and simmer for 20 minutes, or until the meat is tender.

Preheat the oven to 350°F/180°C. Arrange half the eggplant slices in a layer in an ovenproof dish. Add the meat mixture, then a final layer of the remaining eggplant slices.

In a bowl, beat the eggs, then beat in the yogurt, and add salt and pepper. Pour the mixture over the eggplants and sprinkle the grated cheese on top. Bake the moussaka in the oven for 45 minutes, or until golden brown. Serve straight from the dish.

marinated lamb kabobs

		ingredients	
very easy		MARINADE	1 lb/450 g leg of lamb, cut into
		$\frac{2}{3}$ cup lowfat	1 inch/2.5 cm cubes
serves 4		plain yogurt	
		4 tbsp chopped fresh cilantro	chopped fresh parsley, to garnish
		2 tsp chopped garlic	
10 minutes + 2–3 hours to marinate		2 tsp chopped fresh ginger	salad, to serve
		1 tsp ground coriander	
		1 tsp ground cumin	
15–20 minutes		salt and pepper	

NUTRITIONAL
INFORMATION

calories	200
protein	25 g
carbohydrate	3 g
sugars	3 g
fat	10 g
saturates	4 g

Put all the marinade ingredients into a large bowl and mix together. Stir in the lamb until coated in the marinade, then marinate in the refrigerator for 2–3 hours.

Thread the lamb cubes onto metal or bamboo skewers. Cook under a preheated broiler for 15–20 minutes, turning frequently and basting with the marinade, until tender.

Garnish with chopped parsley and serve with salad.

quick-fried pork
& pears

very easy	
serves 4	
15 minutes	
5–7 minutes	

ingredients

1 tbsp soy sauce
1 tsp white wine vinegar
2 tbsp dry sherry
1 lb/450 g pork tenderloin,
   sliced very thinly

2 large pears
4 scallions, sliced thinly
1 tsp chopped garlic
1 tbsp chopped fresh ginger

NUTRITIONAL
INFORMATION

calories	210
protein	25 g
carbohydrate	9 g
sugars	8 g
fat	7 g
saturates	2 g

Put the soy sauce, vinegar, and sherry in a large bowl. Add the pork and mix together. Cut the pears into ¼ inch/5 mm slices, discarding the cores.

Reserve the green part of the scallions to use as garnish. Put the garlic, ginger, and scallions in a large nonstick wok and heat for 1–2 minutes, stirring constantly, until hot.

Add the pork mixture to the wok and stir-fry for 3–4 minutes, or until tender and beginning to brown. Add the pears and stir-fry for a further minute, or until hot.

Serve the stir-fry immediately, sprinkled with the sliced green scallion stems.

vegetarian dishes

Vegetables are the perfect lowfat food and in this section is a collection of recipes using just vegetables as a main course. They illustrate how interesting and varied vegetables can be, but fortunately you don't have to be a vegetarian to enjoy them! You will find lowfat recipes for Cheese & Spinach Lasagna, Vegetable Biryani, Glazed Vegetable Kabobs, and Stuffed Eggplants, among other delicious dishes. Their flavor and freshness have been brought out to the full to provide nutritious and satisfying meals.

spring vegetable risotto

easy	
serves 4	
15 minutes	
30–35 minutes	

ingredients

3¾ cups vegetable bouillon
2 tsp olive oil
1 small leek, sliced thinly
1 tsp chopped garlic
1 carrot, sliced thinly
2 zucchini, sliced thinly
¾ cup snow peas

¾ cup whole green beans,
   cut into 1 inch/2.5 cm pieces
3 cups risotto rice
⅔ cup dry white wine
½ cup frozen baby
   peas, thawed
salt and pepper

NUTRITIONAL
INFORMATION

calories	429
protein	10 g
carbohydrate	36 g
sugars	14 g
fat	16 g
saturates	9 g

Pour the bouillon into a pan, bring to a boil, then keep at barely simmering point.

Meanwhile, heat the oil in a large, nonstick pan, add the leek, garlic, carrot, zucchini, snow peas, and beans and cook, stirring frequently, for 5 minutes, or until beginning to soften but not brown.

Add the rice and stir well for 2–3 minutes, or until coated in the oil. Add the wine and cook, stirring, until almost evaporated.

Add about ⅔ cup of the bouillon and cook gently, stirring occasionally, until absorbed. Add more bouillon, in ⅔ cup measures, as soon as each measure has been absorbed, stirring frequently. Continue until the rice is thick, creamy and tender. This will take 20–25 minutes. Stir in the peas, season with salt and pepper, and serve.

cheese & spinach lasagna

very easy	
serves 4	
15 minutes	
45–50 minutes	

ingredients

1 lb/450 g frozen spinach, thawed
salt and pepper
2 cups lowfat ricotta cheese
8 sheets no-precook lasagna
2¼ cups strained bottled tomatoes

8 oz/225 g reduced fat mozzarella
  cheese, sliced thinly
1 tbsp freshly grated Parmesan cheese

salad (optional), to serve

NUTRITIONAL
INFORMATION

calories	369
protein	23 g
carbohydrate	36 g
sugars	14 g
fat	16 g
saturates	9 g

Preheat the oven to 350°F/180°C.

Put the spinach in a strainer and squeeze out as much excess liquid as possible. Put half in the bottom of an ovenproof dish and add salt and pepper.

Spread half the ricotta over the spinach, cover with half the lasagna sheets, then spoon over half the strained bottled tomatoes. Arrange half the mozzarella slices on top. Repeat the layers and finally sprinkle over the Parmesan cheese.

Bake in the oven for 45–50 minutes, by which time the top should be brown and bubbling.

Serve with salad, if you like.

pasta with ricotta
& sun-dried tomatoes

	very easy	**ingredients**
		12 oz/350 g dried tagliatelle
	serves 4	salt and pepper
		2 cups sun-dried tomatoes
		in oil, drained
	10 minutes	1¾ cups lowfat ricotta cheese
		1 garlic clove, crushed
	10 minutes	

ingredients

12 oz/350 g dried tagliatelle
salt and pepper
2 cups sun-dried tomatoes
 in oil, drained
1¾ cups lowfat ricotta cheese
1 garlic clove, crushed

GARNISH
freshly grated Parmesan cheese
fresh basil leaves

NUTRITIONAL INFORMATION

calories	542
protein	18 g
carbohydrate	74 g
sugars	8 g
fat	22 g
saturates	6 g

Cook the pasta in a large pan of boiling salted water for 10 minutes or as directed on the packet, until tender.

Meanwhile, using scissors, cut the tomatoes into small pieces into a pan. Add the ricotta, garlic, salt, and pepper and heat very gently, without boiling.

Drain the pasta, add to the tomato mixture, and toss together.

Serve garnished with basil leaves and generously sprinkled with freshly grated Parmesan.

penne primavera

ingredients

very easy	
serves 4	
10 minutes	
20 minutes	

1 cup baby corn
½ cup whole baby carrots
salt and pepper
1¼ cups shelled fava beans
generous 1 cup whole green beans,
　cut into 1 inch/2.5 cm pieces
3 cups dried penne

1¼ cups lowfat
　plain yogurt
1 tbsp chopped fresh parsley
1 tbsp chopped fresh chives

a few fresh chives, to garnish

NUTRITIONAL
INFORMATION

calories	398
protein	19 g
carbohydrate	79 g
sugars	11 g
fat	3 g
saturates	1 g

Cook the corn and carrots in boiling salted water for 5 minutes, or until tender, then drain, and rinse under cold running water. Cook the fava beans and green beans in boiling salted water for 3–4 minutes, or until tender, then drain, and rinse under cold running water. If you like, slip the skins off the fava beans.

Cook the pasta in a large pan of boiling salted water for 10 minutes or as directed on the packet, until tender.

Meanwhile, put the yogurt, parsley, chopped chives, salt, and pepper in a bowl and mix together.

Drain the cooked pasta and return to the pan. Add the vegetables and yogurt sauce, heat gently, and toss together, until hot.

Serve garnished with a few lengths of chives.

vegetable biryani

		ingredients	
very easy	1 onion, quartered	1½ cups whole green beans,
	2 garlic cloves	cut into 1 inch/2.5 cm lengths
serves 4	1 tsp chopped fresh ginger	½ cauliflower head, cut into flowerets
	1 tsp ground coriander	1¾ cups basmati rice
	1 tsp ground cumin	2 whole cloves
	1 tsp ground turmeric	¼ tsp cardamom seeds
10 minutes	½ tsp chilli powder	2 tbsp lime juice
	salt and pepper	
	6¼ cups water	chopped fresh cilantro, to garnish
30 minutes	2 carrots, sliced thickly	

NUTRITIONAL
INFORMATION

calories	378
protein	11 g
carbohydrate	80 g
sugars	8 g
fat	2 g
saturates	0 g

Put the onion, garlic, ginger, coriander, cumin, turmeric, chilli, salt, and pepper in a food processor and process until smooth.

Spoon the spice mixture into a large, nonstick pan and cook, stirring, for 2 minutes. Stir in 3¾ cups of the water and bring to a boil. Add the carrots, beans, and cauliflower and simmer for 15 minutes, or until tender.

Meanwhile, put the rice in a strainer and rinse under cold running water. Put in a pan with the remaining 2½ cups of water, the cloves, cardamóm seeds, and salt. Bring to a boil, then simmer for 10 minutes, or until just tender.

Drain the rice and stir into the vegetables with the lime juice. Simmer gently until the rice is tender and the liquid has been absorbed. Serve garnished with cilantro.

bean & vegetable chili

		ingredients	
	very easy	4 tbsp vegetable bouillon	14 oz/400 g canned chopped
		1 onion, chopped coarsely	tomatoes
	serves 4	1 green bell pepper, deseeded	salt and pepper
		and chopped finely	14 oz/400 g canned kidney
		1 red bell pepper, deseeded	beans, drained
		and chopped finely	14 oz/400 g canned black-eye
	10 minutes	1 tsp finely chopped garlic	peas, drained
		1 tsp finely chopped fresh ginger	
		2 tsp ground cumin	chopped fresh cilantro, to garnish
	20 minutes	½ tsp chili powder	
		2 tbsp tomato paste	fresh crusty bread, to serve

NUTRITIONAL
INFORMATION

calories	246
protein	17 g
carbohydrate	44 g
sugars	14 g
fat	2 g
saturates	0 g

Heat the bouillon in a large pan, add the onion and bell peppers and simmer for 5 minutes, or until softened.

Stir in the garlic, ginger, cumin, chili powder, tomato paste, tomatoes (together with their juice), salt, and pepper and simmer for 10 minutes. Stir in the kidney beans and black-eye peas and simmer for a further 5 minutes, or until hot. Remove the pan from the heat and transfer the chili to a warm serving dish.

Garnish with chopped cilantro and serve with fresh crusty bread.

glazed vegetable kabobs

		ingredients	
very easy		⅔ cup lowfat plain yogurt	16 baby corn, halved
			2 zucchini, cut into
serves 4		4 tbsp mango chutney	1 inch/2.5 cm pieces
		1 tsp chopped garlic	16 white mushrooms
		1 tbsp lemon juice	16 cherry tomatoes
15 minutes		salt and pepper	
		8 baby onions, peeled	salad greens, to garnish
10 minutes			

NUTRITIONAL INFORMATION

calories	144
protein	8 g
carbohydrate	26 g
sugars	24 g
fat	1 g
saturates	0 g

Put the yogurt, chutney, garlic, lemon juice, salt, and pepper in a bowl and stir together.

Put the onions in a pan of boiling water. Return to a boil, then drain well.

Thread the onions, corn, zucchini, mushrooms, and tomatoes alternately onto 8 metal or bamboo skewers.

Arrange the kabobs on a broiler pan and brush with the yogurt glaze. Cook under a preheated broiler for 10 minutes, turning and brushing frequently, until golden and tender.

Serve with a garnish of mixed salad greens.

stuffed eggplants

easy	
serves 4	
15 minutes	
45 minutes	

ingredients

2 eggplants
1 onion, chopped finely
1 tsp chopped garlic
1½ cups coarsely chopped
  white mushrooms

2 tsp chopped fresh cilantro
1 cup fresh bread crumbs
salt and pepper
2 oz/55 g feta cheese,
  crumbled finely

NUTRITIONAL INFORMATION

calories	104
protein	5 g
carbohydrate	13 g
sugars	5 g
fat	4 g
saturates	2 g

Put the eggplants in a large pan of boiling water and cook for 20 minutes, or until tender. Drain well.

Cut the eggplants in half lengthwise, scoop out the flesh, and chop finely. Reserve the eggplant shells.

Preheat the oven to 350°F/180°C.

Put the eggplant flesh, onion, garlic, mushrooms, and cilantro in a nonstick skillet and cook for 5 minutes. Stir in the bread crumbs, salt, and pepper.

Stuff the eggplant shells with the mixture and sprinkle with the feta cheese.

Place on a cookie sheet and bake in the oven for 20 minutes. Transfer to warm serving plates and serve immediately.

puddings
& desserts

The lowfat pudding and dessert recipes in
this chapter use fresh or dried fruits and
are bursting with tempting flavors.
There is a selection of both hot puddings
and cold desserts, such as Apple Strudel
with Warm Cider Sauce, Apricot and
Orange Fool, and Raspberry Creams.
Don't forget that old favorite, Fresh Fruit
Salad. Simply use fruits in season and dress
them with your choice of fresh fruit juice.
You will find that all these recipes will
bring an enjoyable finale to any meal.

golden baked
apple pudding

	ingredients
very easy	1 lb/450 g cooking apples
	1 tsp ground cinnamon
serves 4	2 tbsp golden raisins
	4 oz/115 g whole-wheat bread, about
	4 thick slices
15 minutes	generous ½ cup lowfat
	cottage cheese
	4 tbsp light brown sugar
30–35 minutes	generous 1 cup lowfat milk

NUTRITIONAL
INFORMATION

calories	227
protein	5 g
carbohydrate	52 g
sugars	40 g
fat	2 g
saturates	1 g

Preheat the oven to 425°F/220°C.

Peel and core the apples and chop the flesh into ½ inch/1 cm pieces. Put the apple pieces in a bowl and toss with the cinnamon and golden raisins.

Remove the crusts and cut the bread into ½ inch/1 cm cubes. Add to the apples with the cottage cheese and 3 tablespoons of the brown sugar, and mix together. Stir in the milk.

Turn the mixture into an ovenproof dish and sprinkle with the remaining sugar. Bake in the oven for 30–35 minutes, or until golden brown. Serve hot.

apricot & orange fool

	ingredients

extremely easy	generous 1 cup ready-to-eat
	  dried apricots
	1 tbsp honey
	generous 1 cup fresh orange juice
	generous 1 cup lowfat
	  plain yogurt

serves 4	
5 minutes	2 tsp flaked almonds (toasted), to decorate
—	

NUTRITIONAL
INFORMATION

calories	171
protein	6 g
carbohydrate	37 g
sugars	37 g
fat	1 g
saturates	0 g

Put all the ingredients, except the almonds, in a food processor and process until smooth.

Serve in individual glass dishes, decorated with toasted almonds.

spiced baked pears

		ingredients
extremely easy		4 large, firm eating pears
		$\frac{2}{3}$ cup apple juice
serves 4		1 cinnamon stick
		4 whole cloves
		1 bay leaf
5 minutes		
30 minutes		

NUTRITIONAL
INFORMATION

calories	114
protein	1 g
carbohydrate	29 g
sugars	29 g
fat	0 g
saturates	0 g

Preheat the oven to 350°F/180°C.

Peel and core the pears and cut them into quarters. Place in an ovenproof dish and add the remaining ingredients.

Cover the dish and bake in the oven for 30 minutes.

Serve the pears hot or cold.

apple strudel with warm cider sauce

		ingredients	
easy		8 crisp eating apples	SAUCE
		1 tbsp lemon juice	1 tbsp cornstarch
serves 2–4		⅔ cup golden raisins	2 cups hard cider
		1 tsp ground cinnamon	
		½ tsp grated nutmeg	confectioners' sugar, to serve
25 minutes		1 tbsp light brown sugar	
		6 sheets phyllo pastry	
		vegetable oil spray	
15–20 minutes			

NUTRITIONAL INFORMATION

calories	283
protein	3 g
carbohydrate	61 g
sugars	47 g
fat	1 g
saturates	0 g

Preheat the oven to 375°F/190°C. Line a cookie sheet with nonstick liner.

Peel and core the apples and chop them into ½ inch/1 cm dice. Toss the pieces in a bowl, with the lemon juice, golden raisins, cinnamon, nutmeg, and sugar.

Lay out a sheet of phyllo, spray with vegetable oil, and lay a second sheet on top. Repeat with a third sheet. Spread over half the apple mixture and roll up lengthwise, tucking in the ends to enclose the filling. Repeat to make a second strudel. Slide onto the cookie sheet, spray with oil, and bake for 15–20 minutes.

Blend the cornstarch in a pan with a little hard cider until smooth. Add the remaining cider and heat gently, stirring, until the mixture boils and thickens. Serve the strudel warm or cold, dredged with confectioners' sugar and accompanied by the cider sauce.

tropical fruit salad

		ingredients
	very easy	1 ripe mango
		1 papaya
	serves 4	1 small pineapple
		1¼ cups pineapple
		or orange juice
	20 minutes + 1 hour to chill	2 small bananas
	—	

NUTRITIONAL INFORMATION

calories	154
protein	2 g
carbohydrate	38 g
sugars	37 g
fat	1 g
saturates	0 g

Cutting close to the pit, cut a large slice from one side of the mango, then cut another slice from the opposite side. Without breaking the skin, cut the flesh in the segments into squares, then push the skin inside out to expose the cubes, and cut away from the skin. Use a sharp knife to peel the remaining center section and cut the flesh away from the pit into cubes. Reserve any juice and put in a serving bowl with the mango flesh.

Cut the papaya in half and discard the seeds. Remove the skin and cut the flesh into cubes. Peel the pineapple, remove the center core and as many "eyes" as possible, and cut the flesh into chunks. Add both fruits to the mango.

Pour in the fruit juice and chill the mixture in the refrigerator for about 1 hour. Just before serving, slice the bananas and add the slices to the fruit salad.

apple & honey
water ice

		ingredients
	very easy	4 crisp eating apples
		2 tbsp lemon juice
		scant 1 cup water
	serves 4	5 tbsp sugar
		2 tbsp honey
	10 minutes + 5–6 hours to freeze	apple slices, to decorate
	20 minutes	

NUTRITIONAL INFORMATION

calories	175
protein	0 g
carbohydrate	46 g
sugars	46 g
fat	0 g
saturates	0 g

Peel and core the apples and cut them into chunks. Put in a pan with the lemon juice and 1 tablespoon of water and heat gently for about 20 minutes, stirring frequently, until soft.

Meanwhile, put the sugar and the remaining water in a pan and heat gently, stirring, until dissolved. Bring to a boil, then boil for 2 minutes. Remove from the heat.

Push the apple through a strainer into a bowl. Stir in the sugar syrup and honey. Let stand until cold.

When cold, pour the mixture into a freezer container. Freeze, uncovered, for 2 hours until the water ice mixture begins to set. Turn the mixture into a bowl and whisk until smooth. Return to the container and freeze for a further 3–4 hours until firm.

Serve decorated with apple slices.

raspberry creams

	very easy	**ingredients**
	serves 4	2²/₃ cups raspberries ³/₄ cup lowfat cottage cheese 3 tbsp sugar ²/₃ cup lowfat plain yogurt
	10 minutes + 1 hour to chill	confectioners' sugar, to decorate
	—	

NUTRITIONAL
INFORMATION

calories	142
protein	9 g
carbohydrate	25 g
sugars	25 g
fat	1 g
saturates	1 g

Reserving a few whole raspberries to decorate, use the back of a spoon to push the raspberries and cottage cheese through a strainer into a bowl.

Stir the sugar and yogurt into the raspberry mixture and stir to blend, then spoon into individual serving dishes. Chill in the refrigerator for about 1 hour.

Serve chilled, decorated with the reserved raspberries and dusted with sifted confectioners' sugar.

compôte of dried fruit

		ingredients
	extremely easy	1 tbsp jasmine tea
		1¼ cups boiling water
		¼ cup dried apricots
	serves 4	¼ cup dried apple rings
		¼ cup prunes
	25 minutes + 24 hours to marinate	1¼ cups fresh orange juice
	—	

NUTRITIONAL INFORMATION

calories	103
protein	2 g
carbohydrate	25 g
sugars	25 g
fat	0 g
saturates	0 g

Put the tea in a pitcher and pour in the boiling water. Let steep for 20 minutes, then strain.

Put the dried fruits in a serving bowl and pour the jasmine tea and orange juice over them. Cover and marinate in the refrigerator for 24 hours.

Serve the compôte well chilled.

index